Brian Bouldrey

THE PEASANTS AND THE MARINERS

Brian Bouldrey is the author of three novels, *The Genius of Desire*; *Love, the Magician;* and *The Boom Economy*. He has also written the nonfiction books *Honorable Bandit: A Walk Across Corsica*, *Monster: Adventures in American Machismo*, and *The Autobiography Box*, and is the editor of several anthologies. His first Open Door book, *The Sorrow of the Elves*, was published in 2011. Brian teaches writing at Northwestern University.

First published by GemmaMedia in 2013.

GemmaMedia
230 Commercial Street
Boston, MA 02109 USA

www.gemmamedia.com
www.gemmaopendoor.com

Printed in the United States of America

17 16 15 14 13   1 2 3 4 5

978-1-936846-39-9

Library of Congress Cataloging-in-Publication Data

Cover by Night & Day Design

The author gratefully acknowledges the support of Brush Creek Foundation for the Arts Residency Program, where this book was written.

Inspired by the Irish series of books designed for adult literacy, Gemma Open Door Foundation provides fresh stories, new ideas, and essential resources for young people and adults as they embrace the power of reading and the written word.

Brian Bouldrey
North American Series Editor

GEMMA

Open Door

For my mother.

Happiness is not only a hope, but also in some strange manner a memory . . . we are all kings in exile.

—G. K. Chesterton

ONE

Home Surgery

Before we even start our hike on the Ulster Way, a path around the border of Northern Ireland, and certainly long before I read the Ireland guidebook, I make some visits to my pal and fellow hiker Garth at his Chicago condo. We are planning our trip. He lives in a neighborhood called Edgewater, on the top floor of a six-unit brick building which is recognizable among the other buildings on his street because the tuckpointing is a shade whiter. Garth knows that I always show up late, and usually after dark, but what he doesn't know is that I depend on the way the cement between the bricks of his house gleams, like toothpaste.

I am always late, but once I'm ringing the doorbell, I am impatient. I remark on the neighbors' nameplates. "Rob Tarkington Home Surgery," says one. Yuck. "The Boltons" seem to work at home, too, because they have posted instructions for UPS. Everybody is at home but me.

Garth's voice crackles down the intercom, a device that seems old-fashioned to me. "You're late!" he's yelling, and I'm yelling back, "What are you, the narrator?" but I bet he never listens back to enjoy my wit or to make sure I'm not a horrible home surgery patient. I push the inner door to an electrifying and overlong buzz (does Garth think I'm too weak to push open a door? or check my wristwatch?). Climbing to Garth's, I notice a Country Craft sign nestled in fake plastic vines over the Boltons' door on the second floor: "Home Is Where Stories Start."

It will take me a long time to understand that sign. Isn't home the place where the stories end? Certainly, the dreams start at home, or the plans start there, plans that Garth loves to make. We will take as much time planning our trip around the Ulster Way as we do executing it, because that's how Garth is.

I, on the other hand, am aimless, in no hurry to plot a course from point A to point Z, and because of this, I am eternally grateful to Garth. He even plans the planning—a full dinner, guidebooks open to the right pages, pencils, and memo pads. We are going to create an itinerary down to the kind of sandwich we will have for lunch on Tuesday the twenty-third. My only task is to bring the maps.

"Okay," says Garth, just when I think we've planned the trip to death, "Now let's divide up the shared equipment. Who is going to carry the first aid kit?"

"Why don't you get some supplies from creepy Dr. Tarkington?" I suggest. Garth looks at me, not recognizing the name. "Your neighbor? I'm sure he travels light with his—," and here I shudder, "—home surgery kit." I am imagining little bone saws, an awl, lengths of plastic piping that, having provided a conduit for all the body's biles, are lightly rinsed and rolled back into a compact coil, like rope on a ship.

"You are weird. Home surgery does not mean he is going to put you on your kitchen table and pull out rotten teeth with pliers. It means that if something is broken in your home, he will come and fix it."

This, of course, makes more sense. Except that if I were a home surgeon, I would probably call myself a carpenter, or an electrician, or a plumber, or just have a card that had a list of skills. "But you can see how I made that mistake, right?" I make this mistake, thinking of home surgery as something about the self and not about the home, because is a home sick or are we homesick?

All my life I have never been homesick.

I have been sick for away: wanderlust, some call it. I have told myself, whether it is true or not, that if I do not travel all the time, I shall kill myself by staying at home. Ninety-five percent of all accidents occur in the home. And not everybody is lucky enough to live above a home surgery expert. I prefer to take my chances on the road, among all the devils I don't know. "I will carry the first aid kit," I promise.

We unfold the maps, maps made by careful people in France, with a 9:1 ratio. At that level, you can see the homes. They appear as little squares, huddled in towns, lonesome in a world of rivers and roads and turnpikes and trails. Then I realize I have made a mistake. They are maps for the Burren in west Ireland. We are hiking the Ulster Way in Northern Ireland. I have brought the wrong maps. Garth is trying to remain calm, although I have come unprepared, and with the wrong maps. It takes a lot to make Garth mad, but I have made him mad.

I pull a little tin from my pocket. It's filled with hard candies in the shapes of ducks and rabbits. I bought bags of tart candy ducks and bunnies and I keep a handful of them in this little tin. They are my Angry Ducks. I see that Garth is angry, and so I offer him a duck.

"When I'm angry, I put a hard candy duck in my mouth and I suck," I explain. "I don't allow myself to say or do anything until I have sucked the duck until it's gone. By then my anger is usually gone and I don't say or do anything rash. If I am still angry and bite the head off the duck, then I have to start all over again."

Garth puts a duck in his mouth.

"Go ahead," I smile. "Suck that duck."

I hear a cracking noise. Garth says, "I just bit the head off the duck."

"No problem, have another!"

This one lasts longer, about thirty seconds. I am smiling at him and his jaw goes tense. Another crack. He reaches into the tin a third time. "I have an idea—" he starts.

But I caution him. "Do you really want to speak while you're still angry?" He's got a little bunny in his mouth this sorry for the bunny. I

.t you keep sucking on the

. bunnies, and I'll run home

.t the right maps. By the time I get

.ck, you won't be angry and we don't

have to waste any more time before we

continue to plan."

From his silence, I can tell that he likes my plan. He scribbles on a pad of paper, "BRING MORE DUCKS WHILE YOU'RE AT IT." He thinks I'm a bad planner, but see? I have a perfect plan for the next ten minutes.

TWO

The Golden Age of Things

You might wonder how many bags of ducks and bunnies I carried on the bus from Dublin to Belfast, where we begin our walk along the Ulster Way. I will tell you now: a lot of them. Hikers become obsessed with their backpacks, which, like turtle shells, are the homes on their backs. It is amazing what you will place in a bag when you know you will only have those things for an entire month. What a mariner takes on a journey are the things he considers most homely. Think how things weigh heavily upon the body.

And so I am telling you about my-

self when I list the things I carry. Besides the basic equipment of the backpacker (lightweight shirts and shorts and towels made of material that wicks dry with a snap, a tent and a sleeping bag that both roll down to the size of a sandwich, rain-gear, a flashlight, maps, magic pellets that make toilet water an ambrosia fit for a god, the home surgery first aid kit, and a canteen for water), I have taken on the pointless, heavy luxuries of hard candy ducks, a journal, a book with the ridiculous title *The Portable James Joyce*, and five bags of flavored potato chips. As I read the book, I will peel off the pages like the skin of an onion, thinking this will lighten the weight of my pack.

Garth reveals his own character flaws by carrying our well-detailed hiking plan, another guidebook (a heavy one), and a backpack with so many slots and side pockets that it looks like it belongs to a fetishist. There is even a removable satellite pack that must have been designed by somebody who never backpacks, for it sags low and out from the pack, making Garth work harder on the hike. But he is a loyal hiker—he never ditches the heavy pack, the hiking plan he created, or me.

I am taste-testing the new potato chip flavors they never give us back home (Worcester Sauce, Roasted Chicken, Prawn Cocktail, Crispy Duck & Hoisin, Cajun Squirrel). One of the girls from a hen party (we call them bachelorette parties) needs to have a pee, though I am not sure where she thinks she can here, on a

bridge looking over a single man fishing and four other men advising him on how to fish. As she passes me, I let myself sniff her, to see if they're drinking back there and, if so, what they're drinking. But she smells like herbicide—dandelion killer—and not entirely unpleasantly so. I will smell this smell very often over the days ahead. "I can't believe you're eating those crisps," the girl points at my bag. Nobody had a problem with my "Prawn Cocktail" chips, but it seems "Cajun Squirrel" is too much.

I put on my best American accent. "They're exotic," I say, but they are not. "Cajun Squirrel" should be a flavor of my home, where Cajun country is. And where "eatin" squirrels reside. She doesn't want to talk about it. She has to pee. If there are peasants and there are mariners, the hen party is a festival of the peasants.

Garth opens up his itinerary pouch, filled with dates and daily maps he will dispose of each day. He is looking for the place on the map where we are at this moment. He unfolds the down-to-the-farmhouse-ratio Michelin map, using the heads of two Boy Scouts for support. They are oblivious. He is quiet as another hen dismounts with a pack of menthols. Then he says, "We're not even to Newry yet." I don't know what that means, but it's not a good thing for people with agendas.

In all the accounts of travel I have read, not much is said of arrival. If it is spoken of, it is with sadness, as though it were a death, a little death for a lot of

struggle. But when the king arrives in his castle in a play, he is surrounded by noisy fanfare. Doorbells are like fanfare trumpets. When somebody is at the door, the story, the golden age of the king, is just beginning.

"Now I'm thirsty," I tell Garth. He agreed to carry the water if I carried the first aid kit. But he is conserving our water rations, because we didn't realize how long this trip from Dublin to Belfast would last. My feet and tongue swell from eating so many salty chips. I look out at the salty sea.

Garth's head is still buried in the map. "Maybe you shouldn't have eaten all those chips." It's the way he says it that makes me pull out an Angry Duck. Both Garth and I are teachers—we have taught a class together, one on food and politics. He taught on Tuesdays and I taught on Thursdays. There were two separate lesson plans. Can you imagine what they looked like?

Then he looks up, and you can see the whites of his eyes. "Why didn't you tell me we were going to be hiking within three miles of the Bushmills whiskey distillery?" He grabs my empty potato chip bag and uses it for trash. And by trash, I mean the pages of our itinerary.

THREE

The Peasant and the Mariner

Two days later, we are standing on the road next to the sign that bids you farewell from Bushmills, County Antrim, Northern Ireland. "Take a picture of me sprawled on the road in front of the sign with this bottle of whiskey!" Garth hands me his ridiculously large camera. It weighs as much as the water bottle, or my five bags of hard candy ducks, and is a "gift" from his sister. He wants to look like the town drunk. We have just toured the Bushmills distillery, which is a big high barn with the words "Old Bushmills Distillery" tiled into the roof, a sort of lighthouse for the blind drunk.

Garth wants us all to think he is a lush. But, as my mother would say, it's the loud ones you don't have to worry about. Nevertheless, I shoot at least a dozen pictures of my excellent companion pretending he's having to hold on to the grass to keep from falling off the earth.

He is sorry for it when he realizes the grass he didn't have to hold on to is nettles. There are a lot of nettles in County Antrim. The sting of nettles is curious. Earlier in the day, I had come across a fence made of a single thin wire that surrounded pastureland for cows. Through the wire the farmer had sent a weak but real electrical current, enough to keep the cattle from wandering off on an incredible unwanted journey. I had rested my hands on the wire for a full five seconds before the tingle of the charge finally registered as electrification. I pulled my hands away as if I'd had them stuck in a hornet's nest. Nettles have the same charge, but once you pull your hands off the nettles, the electrification continues. In fact, it grows stronger.

I reach for his stage prop, the beautiful (and heavy, for a hiker) bottle of Black Bush and tell him that the topical application of whiskey is excellent for killing off the sting of nettles. "Don't you dare!" Garth, sitting against a rock, recoils into a fetal ball. Nettles hurt.

Below us, a fisherman throws his line in, and his two advisers direct him to throw again. Everybody, whether they are a peasant or a mariner or a fisherman with one foot on shore and one at sea, is full of wise sayings, and wise-assing.

What does a walker do when he stops walking? He gets restless. He wants to be on his way, so that he can be alone with his thoughts, even if he is walking with a friend. And what does a walker think about when alone with his thoughts? I, for one, think about home. Not in a longing way, but in the way that suggests that home is as wild and independent of me as nature. It is something that is both outside myself where I seek truth, and inside myself, where I seek beauty. Truth and beauty: good reasons for walking alone on a trail, knowing you will have a wee dram or three with your good organized nettled friend at the end of the day.

I have walked alone together with friends for many years. Walking has whittled my legs and heart into durable pieces of hardened human furniture.

But hardness is not always a quality in me. I don't need to tell you that, after a while, alone becomes lonesome, single-mindedness becomes selfishness, and impatience becomes anger. That's why I carry Angry Ducks. I want to conquer all my fears. There are reasons why we have fears, I learned. Fear keeps us from destroying ourselves. But still—wherever I have traveled, the great moments worth writing about seem to come when I am unhomed, alone. I do think it's important for people to know how to be alone, alone with God, alone with the wisdom of the road or of the past.

But alone is different from lonely, just as much as grief is different from grievance. It's the difference between saying "I am interested" and saying, instead, "I am interesting."

In the Bible, the return home is symbolic of the soul's return to God. And aren't mariners supposed to give us the lore of faraway places, to share their knowledge from the open road? The ants are morally superior to the grasshopper. In the Book of Job, Satan wanders about the earth and God stays put. To ramble on, partying hearty and cruising the avenue and shirking responsibilities of family—that is what the Prodigal Son did, and that will put you deep in the bowels of H-E-double-hockey-sticks.

I have walked across many wide

open spaces, and traveled to nearly every country in Europe. I have walked twice through romantic France and Spain to Santiago de Compostela. I have climbed around in the sublime Italian Dolomites and Swiss Alps and walked across the island of Corsica. But there is another kind of landscape, neither sublime nor romantic, but never drab. It is soothing and nondescript, something that rolls like ocean forever and forever from your view. It is green and regular. It is Ireland. It is my homeland. I have seen so much of the world, but I saved the place where most of my ancestors come from because I was not excited about paying for an expensive plane ticket that would bring me to home, the place where stories start, and end.

Ireland looks exactly the way I thought it would. Ireland is a thing you use to compare other places to, because everybody knows what you're talking about, even if they haven't been to Ireland. "What do the Azores look like?" a friend asked me after I had gone hiking there along the lip of a dead volcano that had erupted inside a deader volcano. "If Ireland and Hawaii had a baby, it would look like the Azores," I said. My friend understood. An Irish person would understand. Don't you?

"What are you thinking about?" asks Garth, who is feeling no pain, nettlesting or otherwise, after a couple of Guinness pints in the closest pub. It's quiet. There are sports on the telly, but nothing to bet on, not here, anyway, so we are nearly the only ones in the place.

I suddenly grab my pocket tin for a hard candy duck, and suck. Garth sees this. He reverently waits for the duck to melt away in my mouth. Then he says, "What are you so angry about this time?"

Thinking of home, and the sea being wide, and not being able to swim over, I say, "I just want to tell my mother that I wouldn't sashay so much if she didn't have so many tchotchkes."

Garth looks at me. He holds out his hands. I give him a duck. He says, "You are very weird," and then he puts the duck in his mouth.

FOUR

The Prodigal Son

A few days up the road from the thicket of nettles and the Bushmills distillery is the town of Portrush, where we stay the next night. There is a hostel for backpackers run by Mrs. Josephine McShane. She likes us because we have so much in common.

"I have a son who lives in Chicago. Shane."

You know, Shane. McShane. "Shane McShane." I can't stand not saying it out loud.

"Then you know him?" his mother asks. "He lives in that one neighborhood in Chicago, you know, the one where the O'Shea girl got beat up. *You* know, the O'Shea girl."

I screw up my eyes trying to recall something I can't recall because I never knew it in the first place. I name half a dozen bad neighborhoods. No. We are still standing with our backpacks hanging off our weary shoulders, and they are heavy and Garth is itching. We have to come up with Shane's neighborhood, like a password. I offer half a dozen more, neighborhoods affordable to students and new Americans. Nope. I can hear the hiss of a lovely warm shower falling on somebody else down the hall. I give Mrs. McShane the names of a half-dozen nice neighborhoods in Chicago, including my own and Garth's. Nope.

I sigh. "I am sorry, ma'am, but there

are a *lot* of beatings in Chicago." I say we are a violent people. This fact seems to satisfy her. She leads us to the men's bunks.

And Garth adds under his breath, after she leaves, "Usually the beatings are done by *your* people."

"My people? Or her people?" He is already in the shower, scrubbing his newest wounds. Garth is not Irish, but of Welsh extraction. We both sunburn easily.

Who are "my" people? I am still standing there in my full backpack. In all my mariner past, I have stomped and sailed and trained through more than thirty nations and nationalisms, twenty islands and provinces, and all but one of the fifty American states. I plop my backpack on a chair as if I am about to move in. In none of those places, not even the place where I was born, have I said, as I do at this moment, sweaty, dirty, nettled, weary, "This is home." Well, I said it once, about one other place.

"Excuse me," says a hiker guy in a thick German accent, "but this is my chair you are using." Such a polite boy! We are wild people on the road. Why do we walk? The same reason we drink, or wear masks during carnivals. Aren't we always looking for a socially acceptable way to be socially unacceptable? And isn't *socially unacceptable* another word for crazy? Prodigal? Home is the opposite of crazy. When we want to leave home, then the place we want to go is crazy.

FIVE

We Are Kings in Exile

The German boy is tall. Very tall. Tall like a giant. Which is funny because we are going to hike the Giant's Causeway, and we are trying to convince the giant hiking boy to join us. He is trying to decide. He looks like he is always thinking hard about something, although not something going on right in front of him. Or he is thinking of something that is going on right in front of us, but I can't see it. He looks like he is thinking about something other than the conversation we are having with him. It doesn't seem rude; yet it is as if his body is so tall and many-parted that it requires that his mind be elsewise engaged on some complicated, necessary activity, like dancing a bossa nova or waiting for a chess opponent to make his move.

"We are going in the same direction. Do you want to walk with us?"

Can somebody look both afraid and brave at the same time? This is a hiker's very essence, and it makes us look . . . unnatural. Certainly the German boy, whose name is Gerhardt, sticks out like a sore thumb. But I have no right to talk. I try to blend in when I am traveling, but I am given away by my maps, my backpack, my eyes the sizes of saucers as I oh-my-God my way through the new wonderful landscape. Since I feel both afraid and brave at the same time, I also look like two different people: my blundering self, and my blundering people.

Perhaps this is where prejudice is born. If you try to make a foreign place your home, the locals think that not just you, but all the reputed weaknesses of your culture have moved in, too. There goes the neighborhood. When I am walking my dog in the park, you may scowl, for you do not see a dog and his master, but every pile of unshoveled dog doo you have ever stepped in. I assure you that this dog owner steps in just as much dog doo as you do.

I know nothing about Gerhardt except that he is German, tall, and hiking in Ireland. He has taken up both chairs next to our bunks in Mrs. McShane's small hostel, and I draw my own conclusion from the limited information I have. He has taken up all the available space, and that is because he is a German who needs his *lebensraum*. Next thing you know, he'll be taking over Poland. After I think this, I feel very bad for thinking it. But I won't lie: I think it. And I also want one of those chairs so I can sit and put on my clean socks.

But Gerhardt needs all this room because his entire home is in his backpack. Besides the clothing and tent and cooking utensils, he has his laptop and speakers, and is that a mixing board? He is upset because the hostel has no Wi-Fi. He is also upset because he has too many things from home in his backpack, and he does not feel very much at home.

Is this what he is thinking about? Perhaps his English is as terrible as my German. I know how to say, "Get out of that bed!," "You are as red as a lobster!," and "black bathing suit." I say all these things to him and he is convinced I am fluent in his language.

"Do you want to walk with us tomorrow? We will cross the rope bridge and we will walk by the Giant's Causeway."

The Giant's Causeway is one of the most famous places in Ireland, and in the world. Thousands of black stone hexagonal pillars cleave together at the water's edge in Antrim and create a sort of bridge that reaches out toward Scotland and into the sea. There is a story of an actual giant, an Irish one named Finn McCool, who was challenged by another giant across the water, which was then spanned by a complete causeway. When Finn saw this other giant, he became both frightened and brave, and he ran into his house, dressed like a baby, and hid in a baby crib. When the Scottish giant saw Baby Finn, he thought, "If this is what their babies look like, what must the adults look like?" and he ran in fear across the causeway back to Scotland, smashing the bridge into fragments. This is what Garth, Gerhardt, and I hike past. Travelers are always running away in fear or coming here to conquer.

Gerhardt never said he would walk with us, and, in fact, he seemed to say that he was walking in the other direction, but for more than half a day he hikes with us, stands in line to cross a precarious rope bridge that connects two pillars of stone, and laughs at our jokes, even when they aren't funny. He is always looking at the Irish sky full of clouds that are like meringue and battlefield cannon smoke, or thinking about a chess move, or mentally rehearsing the bossa nova footwork.

Garth keeps trying to plan the next day, but Gerhardt keeps saying goodbye to us, always leaving us, but never leaving. It is as if we are his chess opponents, and all our moves are strategies he is trying to uncover and outwit.

And then I see the ice cream man. "Ooh, look, it's Mr. Whippy!" I shout. I run off the trail, because ice cream is just as much a goal for me as getting away or going home. And this, after all the tension of the German boy's day-long decision-making, is what makes him realize that we aren't trying to take him in a game of chess. I have broken the spell of seriousness, and Gerhardt is free. We were just fooling around. Wandering around. He immediately says goodbye, and the last we see of him he is heading toward a simple white church surrounded by a pretty little graveyard at the top of a hill. It is as if we, too, were under a spell. Where is Gerhardt going? He is taller than the church. He is a giant and he is a baby. He is afraid and he is brave. He is at home and abroad.

SIX

The Prodigal Son's Party

"Britt!!! Why are't you now be here? You broke me! You are so special and drunk! I am beautiful and today Brian and I BUSHMILL!"

We are in Coleraine. Garth is on his second round of whiskey and is writing postcards as if he were drunk-dialing old girlfriends back home. He signs the card to Britt—who is, by the way, married and expecting a child at any moment—with a signature and a smiley face that has a mustache instead of a smile.

I'm sticking to Guinness tonight. I am technically the soberest person in the room, but I don't grade on a curve. He's left a space at the bottom for me, the "designated postcarder," since I'm stout-totaling. This leaves me the tasks of apologizing for his behavior on the card and addressing it in legible handwriting. "I'm afraid our little friend had a wee dram too much of the local," I write. I don't have to explain to Britt that "Bushmill" is not a verb.

We are celebrating the last night walking along the glorious coast before we hike inland. We have drunk more than our fair share of the Bushmills. And of the Guinness. We found a Guinness ice cream man, a tinkling truck with taps in the flatbed. We have come looking for real things tonight, and we intend to find them in this old tavern.

We want to hear live trad music, and

we've secured a good table near the fireplace where the band lounges—three sullen boys, really, and a tagalong girlfriend who may or may not sing, we're not sure. Even in the oldest tavern in Ireland, I am the Designated Postcarder, but I am slugging down Guinness much more quickly than I ought to, replacing my body's waters with this, the gift of the Guinness toucan.

It doesn't help that I keep buying packets of peanuts that are clipped to a cardboard display of a naked lady, each packet covering an important unmentionable part of her body. I keep going up and buying a Guinness and a packet of peanuts, but the bartender is blind to my goal. There's no guarantee that the girl on the cardboard peanut display

is completely naked under those peanuts, but hope springs eternal. I am as
bold as beer can make me, so I shout
over the pennywhistle and the drum
that are finally starting up by the fireplace: "Could you possibly give me a bag
from the chestal area?" The bartender
either can't hear or can't understand my
American English, which I understand
sounds to them like a cat chewing gum.
I point to the peanut lady, though, and
he smiles, finger on his nose. He pulls
off a bag of peanuts from the left tata
zone, to reveal . . . *another bag of peanuts*.
It's a shell game, and I've been taken,
like so many tourist rubes before me.
I leave an extra crown on the bar anyway. I will humiliate this bar with my
American magnanimity. They will prove

not to care. This is another bitter beauty of travel: not being the center of one's own universe.

The bar is starting to fill up, and the boys begin to play. The girl, we discover, is just there for decoration. It's easy to guess that the young lady is a new distraction—the boy who plays the Irish drum has only recently hooked up with her, probably the night before. He is wearing his very best beat-up old T-shirt with E.T. the Extraterrestrial on it. She keeps pawing him, and the other two band members resent the living hell out of her. Did she make him miss rehearsal? She reclines, taking up most of a bench, making the boys clump together. Her head is nearly inside her boyfriend's *bodhran*, one of those shallow Irish drums, but she seems oblivious to the fact that they are playing music, frisky Irish music. I am fascinated by the way she can, in the midst of all this music that makes me move my feet and bob my head, be lazily texting on her smartphone. They're singing "The Star of the County Down."

> I've travelled a bit, but never was hit
> Since my roving career began
> But fair and square I surrendered there
> To the charms of young Rose McCann.

Now, I know this song. I have danced to this song at drunken *ceilidhs* in Cape Breton, office parties in San Francisco, living rooms in Barcelona, classrooms in Chicago. But this vital tune, like any animal taken from its native habitat, when it does not look incongruous or defanged, looks forlorn. It looks as though it were away from its lover, a reluctant mariner rather than a voluntary one, a soldier drafted for somebody else's war, a vagabond looking for work.

To be here, here in a room with this song, with these boys, not one of them yet eighteen years old (but still the obliging bartender slides the pints down the bar to their end, where they sit below and surreptitiously reach over their heads now and then, intuiting that another glass has appeared there for them), it's a revelation. Like coming out of Plato's cave into true light.

The boy in moldy dreadlocks (he didn't anticipate that the cold Irish wet would make him reek more than his Jamaican counterparts; let us call the poor boy Ras Casey) plays a frolicking pennywhistle, as if there were any other kind. The other, who is all business on the banjo, the mandolin, and anything else with five strings that he can get his hands on, can sing "Dublin" into a four-syllable word. He is short, and wears high tops that end near his knees. We are momentarily blinded by a flash that comes out of the camera in the girl's phone—stage-eye-view of the audience. She slips back toward her boyfriend's crotch.

"It's like she wants to be that drum," Garth observes.

"It's like she wants to be Yoko Ono," I say.

I'll tell me ma when I get home,
The boys won't leave the girls alone!

They are singing, "She is handsome, she is pretty! She is the belle of Belfast City!" I love a people who can describe a beautiful woman as handsome, but then, I have always found it sexy when boys are given girls' names and girls given boys' names—Jo in *Little Women*, and her true love Laurie.

Albert Mooney says he loves her!
All the boys are fighting for her!

The songs they play are all traditional, but they are also emphatic—feisty, full of a prowling tension, like a pint of still-tapped stout with too much head, or a banana peel on the floor in front of a barback carrying all the empty pint glasses. But declarative, as if the barback had seen the banana peel, stopped in front of it, and thrown all the glasses to the floor with a grand gesture: "THERE!"

Let them all come as they will!
It's Albert Mooney she loves still!

The song goes out with drumming-fingers-on-the-drum drumming, and even Yoko has to climb out from under the song's spirit. When the sweat moon from his T-shirt collar has spread to E.T.'s glowing finger, Lothario stops, and all three boys head out the door for a fag break, because even Coleraine observes the no smoking signs. There is nothing to replace their presence or sound but three flyblown portraits of what were probably important Irish poets a couple of hundred years ago.

"Alas, I don't recognize a single one of them," I tell Garth, who asks whether I recognize any of the dead poets' society. *Alas* is a word used only by poets, or by a person who is writing you a letter of rejection.

I am ready for another designated Guinness. Garth gently points out that Bushmills makes a ginger ale. Just as I'm about to stand up, a shadow looms over the two of us. "Have any room, don't you?" comes a booming brogue. Our table is tiny, painted black to hide a half-century's graffiti—political graffiti. You can still see a few key words dug in so deep with a penknife, or with fervor and hurt as sharp as a penknife, that can never be painted over. "Loughgall." "Our day will come." But the most important thing about the table is that it is tiny. And pretty much covered with empty pints, shot glasses, and Garth's drunken postcards.

But we are guests here, and don't know the ways—or even, for that matter, what it is he said, exactly, because his Irish is so thick. "Sure there's room." Down they sit, big guy and little guy. Hammer and Nail. Now I can't get up to get another pint, which I have never wanted more in my life.

"I'm Brian, and this is Garth."

The big one says, "I'm Big Jim. And this here is Little Gerry." There is nothing ironic about their names. "In our country, we'd call you Tiny, Big Jim!"

Big Jim is as unironic as his name. He is a sincere man. Do you want to know what sincere people have no patience for? Irony.

Little Gerry is studying his cell phone and says something that has a question mark on the end. I guess. "We're from the United States, Chicago."

"We love your country," Garth adds, just in case.

"No no no," Big Jim has interpreted Little Gerry's inscrutable accent. "He wants to know what you're doing here."

"We're looking around," I say. "My family is Irish, mostly. This is my homeland."

That's when Little Gerry snaps his phone shut like your finger was caught in it.

But Big Jim is furious, too. I thought he would like to know that we are brothers, bras, and share Ireland as a homeland. I am wrong, it seems. Through his teeth, Big Jim says, "He thinks we should all step outside."

I am pretty sure "stepping outside" is a universal expression for "bar fight." I have never been in a bar fight before. I have no training. Besides liquor. But I told you about the sort of drunk I am. I am a "here's my wallet, have a ball!" drunk. But my wallet is empty—we had a lot of Guinness. I pull out my little tin. I almost suggest, "Suck on our ducks! We'll all feel better." But I think better of it.

Now they are both standing, towering over us, madder than ever. What did I say? What did I say?

But none of this matters. Because by the time we get to the next chapter, I will be mincemeat in some alley in Coleraine. Home is also the place where you feel you can die. My affairs are in order.

Garth, who has many sorts of itineraries, looks at me not with horror, but with glee. This is on his bucket list: dying in a bar fight.

SEVEN

The Prodigal Son's Homecoming Party Bar Fight

Little Gerry says words, fighting words. Out of habit, I turn to Big Jim for a broken translation, but Big Jim is done translating.

"Why do you come here," Big Jim asks, "to buy up all our land so we have nowhere to live? This is our country."

What? I never said that. "We aren't going to buy your land," I say. And it occurs to me that these guys heard me say "homeland" and concluded that I was here to buy real estate. "I don't even own land in the States! I don't even approve of owning land! I'm just a teacher hiking the Ulster way with my teacher friend!"

I am ready to move on to the subject that would start a bar fight in nearly any bar in the world: I don't consider the ownership of land the definition of home. Maybe you do. But I think "a place to die" is a less flimsy definition for home, personally.

Big Jim drops his dukes. "Oh, Gerry, never ya mind! Ya don't want to talk the real estate with'em, they're on holiday! It's two schoolteachers on holiday."

Little Gerry's face sags and reforms in an instant, like wedding cake frosting propped back up with a spatula. He pockets his phone the way you sheath a knife. He puts a wiry, wired hand on Garth and says, just momentarily understandable, "I almost bashed yer face in with a hurley stick. That would have been hilarious. Let me buy you a Guinness."

"Just like that," Garth mutters to me.

I don't think Gerry hears him as he marches up to the bar. He marches back with four pints of Harp, one for each of us. Perhaps he realized that Guinness is more expensive than Harp. "Pull me off 'em!" he says to Big Jim, and whether he meant the beers or the boys, I did not press.

And that's right about the time when the band members came in from their various businesses, and Yoko was not among them. Everybody seemed more at ease. And somewhere along the way, somebody had bought the key bag of peanuts, and we all had a good time looking at the wardrobe malfunction on the naked lady from Treetz & Co.

It's a bit sad to me that the people I really want to discuss home with—like Big Jim and Little Gerry, like Garth's neighbors who indulge in home surgery and stories that begin at home, like my mother—wouldn't know how to have the conversation. It's in their bodies, not their mouths. I envy people who feel at home in the world in the way that I envy people with a natural sense of direction, or perfect pitch—a natural talent.

People in Ireland have a low regard for people in the States who put "Kiss Me I'm Irish" bumper stickers on their cars. "Plastic Paddys" is what they call them. In grade school, everybody was expected to wear green on Saint Patrick's Day, or suffer the punishment of crowd-sourced pinching. When my mother laid out my clothes for school one Saint Patrick's Day morning and I had not a kelly color to wear, she hugged me and told me that, "You don't have to wear green, because you're Irish. It's like wearing green every day of your life." My mother did not raise me to be a Plastic Paddy. And I came home with welts, from all the pinching because I didn't wear green that day.

Most of my immigrant grandparents wanted to forget all the troubles and famines and bad luck of the Irish. In Ireland, I can see myself in every reflective surface. Especially the surface of a repainted table in White's Tavern, with beer rings and peanut-skin flakes and gouged-out graffiti about the IRA. Big Jim and Little Gerry, you're me bra's. Even though you don't give a damn, and I can't understand a word you say.

EIGHT

The Prodigal Son's Mom

A week later, we hike into Belfast, the end of the Ulster Way. You cannot make homemade things until you've made a home. That's why I was so careful to select this home, a large one near the University of Belfast that is something like a bed and breakfast, but with more rooms. Now, at two in the morning on a Saturday night, Garth and I are snug in our beds. We are facing each other across the room and are blessed with an over-wrought vanity table with a mirror that captures and magnifies and duplicates city light so much that the room is nearly as bright as daylight. And somebody is unlocking our door from the hallway.

We should have seen this coming. I had made a reservation for this room from a guidebook that said we should book ahead for weekends, and this was a weekend. Now yes, it's sad that the two of us would be in our beds sound asleep on a Saturday night, but our nerves were jangled from the bar fight we had nearly had, and we both had summer colds. Garth had it first, and then I caught it, but I'm not holding a grudge.

But I digress. When we arrived at the door of this home away from home, it took us several rings, those clarion trumpets announcing the arrival of kings and vagabonds. No answer. "We Require Payment in Advance," said the friendly placard on the door. We were about to hike our weary selves down the hill to find other accommodations when a young woman opened the door, looking furtive, as if we were parents who had just caught the babysitter we'd hired making out with her boyfriend on the couch.

"We made a reservation for two," I said. She jumped around as if everything were in order, although she did not ask to see our passports, did not ask for payment in advance. She also didn't show us to our room. She took us into the living room, which was strewn with dozens of outdated and ratted travel magazines and torn maps. Nothing was newer than journals dated two years prior.

We were still standing there, tired

and sweaty, in our backpacks. This was becoming a theme. Did we not look tired enough? A motormouth even among a people proud to have the gift of the gab, the woman was describing the breakfast service, threaded with an account of how she loved the travel writer Arthur Frommer because he had written good things about the hotel, when I interjected, "We're pretty beat after a long day of hiking. Could you show us our room?"

Then she fell all over herself again and just grabbed a key from a board and took us to the first available room in the hall. One of the beds was still unmade, but clean, cheap sheets were folded there, ready. I ended up making the bed myself later.

This is a family-run hotel. We show

up in the morning for the Ulster Fry, the sort of breakfast you'd have for dinner in the States: bacon, eggs, sausage, soda bread, beans, some more sausages. It is given to us by the only competent member of the staff, a pudgy gay boy who has clearly spent the last two nights at the disco, and who is yet the last one standing. What keeps him upright? Willpower? And why does it always look as if the entire family has been eating powdered-sugar doughnuts?

Now, I know that in most homes, guests, like fish, begin to smell after three days, but here in the wee hours, I am reminding myself that this is only our second night. And we mean to pay. Somebody is fiddling with the locked door, and the fact that they don't have the key or are unable to handle the key is the only reason why they are not standing in the mirror-lit room right now.

Garth is the first to say something. "Hello?"

From outside the door is a shocked silence. Then, "Somebody is *in* there."

"Yes," I say. "Paying guests."

Sounds of footfalls racing down the hallway. I'm sure it was a ghost.

We have connections to make in the late morning, and we try to check out of our haunted house of ghosts covered in white powder. More ghosts come floating in and flying out, pale, wraithlike, eyes like saucers. We have been sleeping in a crack house.

And what's worse: we cannot seem to find anybody who will take our money.

Garth is an honest man. I am a man who knows about drug use. "I say we go," say I.

"We can't go without paying!"

We sit among the shredded magazines in the front room and wait. I see that the flowers in the vase, which I had taken for fresh, are silk, and faded in the sun. Somebody made an effort to make this room cozy, but that was long ago. A room is not a house, and a house is not a home. We compromise: if the big hand is on the nine and the little hand is near the twelve, then we grab our backpacks and we leave. They never took our passports, despite regular attempts to thrust them into their hands.

At noon, we walk out the door. I turn back for just a moment, like Lot's wife, and understand that the sign, "We Require Payment in Advance," is not a reminder for guests, but for the hosts.

There are 188 named women in the Bible, mostly in the "begats." There are a couple of queens, and a prophetess or two, but the ones with any character at all have the qualities of a shrieking harridan, if not those of a Jezebel or a Magdalene. "Curse God and die," says Job's wife, Dinah, a shriek of reason among the pottery shards and dead daughters. At the very best, a good Bible wife is a silent Bible wife—happy to go along with whatever crazy-assed idea the boys come up with. Building an ark, killing their firstborn, blowing up Sodom. Sure, whatever! I always wondered what the Prodigal Son's mother did when he finally skulked back into the house. "Hi, Mom. I'm home. Dad says you need to go and kill the fatted calf and open some bags of Prawn Cocktail chips, because we're having a party in my honor."

I see her already draining the calf, and motioning to the cutting board—*you're going to have to help me.* "Start chopping veggies. I only have two hands." This is what my mother does when I come home for the holidays—puts me to work. And I am grateful for that. Home is not standing on ceremony, especially when preparing for the ceremony. In my mother's home, if I cook the turkey, the turkey I make is homemade. Even if it's not my home.

My friend John once asked his mother for her rice pudding recipe, a family favorite. How much rice do I use? "As much as you have." And how much milk do I pour in? "As much as you want." And how much sugar? "As much as you need." And how long do I cook it? "Until it's done." That is home, made: as much as you have, as much as you want, as much as you need, until it's done.

NINE

Ireland Looks Exactly the Way You Think It Does

"That's the way I expected Ireland to look," says Garth, remembering how we rounded a set of tufa cliffs and saw: a golf course. A golf course that ended without our realizing it and became a green, green field for a herd of cows. Tufts of super-green, overlong grass grew on a lighter green field where cowplops had over-fertilized the earth. And the farmer's field ended, too, without our noticing it, because the sparse cemetery it became was just as green. Just exactly the way we thought it would be. Garth is a little disappointed, because he thought the accents would be thicker.

"Are you kidding me? Little Gerry might as well have been speaking Basque."

We are on the bus back to Dublin, to catch a flight back home, to our home. I love hearing the way Garth tells the stories of our adventures. We are already telling the stories of what happened on this trip, and we haven't even ended the trip yet. Home is the place where stories start. There's the golf course. "It looks like Ireland," Garth said. So does the pasture. So does the cemetery.

The wife and heiress of the man who invented the Winchester rifle was haunted by the victims of that gun, who directed her to build a house according to their instructions. The dead souls came to her in a dream, and so she spent her life building a dream house, the Winchester Mystery House. Over the years, she added stairs that went nowhere, doors that did not open. Think of who the early victims of the Winchester were—Native Americans, robbers on the run, wandering varmints. Folks not exactly concerned or experienced with building a sensible house.

There is wisdom in the Chinese *Book of Odes*: "Useless to ask a wandering man/Advice on the construction of a house./The work will never come to completion."

Home is a haunted house. Full of unfulfilled promises, curtailed dreams, things under the bed and in the closet, phones that start ringing for no reason, stairways leading nowhere. "There is only one way to appease a ghost," writes Irish writer Patrick Pearse, "you must do what it asks you." We have come in the wake of the "Tiger," that great boom before the great bust, and there are versions of the Winchester Mystery House all over Ireland, high-rises unfinished, doors that step off into space, unrented apartments, faded banners that read, "Future Home of Luxury Condos."

Beyond the golf course and the cow pasture, beyond these you will find the Belfast cemetery. Why are cemeteries always a traveler's destination? My friend Joanne warned me not to tell the locals you are on a genealogy mission because they will never leave you alone. They will take you right up to your dead great-granny and tell you the whole story about how she would keep her dentures loose in her mouth and roll them in there, a nervous tic. How she would suddenly slide them into place so that she could be clearly heard when she shouted, "Fooking Prots!" I never knew this woman, but I know for a fact she was family.

Shelter, house, home, homeland. That last word ought to carry with it all the heartfelt heartiness of home, but something about "homeland" is too big to keep warm. "How much does it cost to keep this homeland heated in winter?" somebody from the tour group wants to know.

We dream—as we go through the airport customs—alone. But we always make sure we take a friend to the cemetery. It was the last thing Garth and I did together before returning. That's where we started telling stories before the travel was even done. Bar fights, crack houses, nettles, Bushmilling, Yoko Ono. We tell our ancestors all these things, sitting on headstones.

In those stories, it's Garth and me, a backpack, and Cajun Squirrel-flavored chips between the wide open skies over Carrickfergus and the sawgrass cutting at our legs as we look over the sea. It's so clear I can see part of Scotland from here, and I think of the story of Finn McCool.

TEN

Tallulah

As the wise man Walter Benjamin put it, all storytellers come from two tribes: the mariners and the peasants. We listen to the stories of the sailors for "the lore of faraway places, such as a much-traveled man brings home." We hear the stories of the peasants for "the lore of the past, as it best reveals itself to natives of a place." Is it possible to be both a peasant and a mariner?

I would like you to believe that my stories are those of the mariner, and that I have wisdom to impart from the road, from the long sea crossings. From other lands. From new friends. Just as

I can assure you that my mother, who has always lived in the town where she bore me, has many great stories from the past—*my* past. A past I sometimes wish to forget.

There is a tale my mother tells like a ghost story every Christmas night (after opening the single bottle of Lancers that she sips through the entire calendar year). It involves a load of snow-white underwear (she had three sons and my father, so it was a lot of underwear) fresh from the washing machine, destroyed by some mysterious crook who placed a large box of crayons into the dryer with them. Who, as they say, dunnit? The story has been told so many times that we have probably wiped out any telltale details that could lead to a conviction. I personally think it was an accident: somebody puts something on top of something else, hiding that first thing, and off it all goes, somethings, to another place, and this particular place a hot dryer. This happens in my own home all the time. But I love to listen to my mother tell this story, and I hope somebody might stand up and finally, after thirty-five years, admit the mistake.

I have always listened to my mother. She carries the wisdom that matters for living among the devils you know. For example, I always ate my beets. I never eat cookie dough because it will give me worms. I usually put the toilet seat down. I have never turned my eyelids inside out, for fear that they might stay that way. You can't kiss a hemorrhoid to make it feel better. At least put on lipstick! Eat hot soup on a hot day so that the air around you feels cooler. Don't talk to old Mr. Moulton, he is crazy. You like the name "Tallulah"? Then you've been hanging around too many ethnic people. You're a terror to rats. My spaghetti sauce calls for three *cloves* of garlic, not three *bulbs*. Walk quickly and don't make eye contact. Make sure when you visit Marshall Field's that you leave out the same door you went in, otherwise you'll get lost. Your taste is all in your mouth. If you read too much, it will fill your head with dangerous ideas. You wouldn't knock over so many of my tchotchkes if you didn't sashay so much.

I have listened to my mother because I have always wanted to have both kinds of knowledge, that of the mariner and that of the peasant. I wanted that knowledge the way only an impatient single-minded adventurer—one who travels best on foot, nothing to pull him down, on his own—is hungry for all knowledge.

And I wanted to bring knowledge from faraway lands. These are things I know about living with the devil you don't know: Roll your clothes to avoid wrinkles. Always check the bed-and-breakfast host's ankles for flea and bedbug bites. Wash the travel utensils with which you've had oatmeal in cold river water. Always have a good story to tell when you begin the haggling in the bazaar, it's part of the business. A butch in the streets is a femme in the sheets.

Papa was a rolling stone, and all he left you was alone. Here's a man who lives a life of danger. Everywhere he goes, he stays a stranger. If the baby is that big, then imagine how big the adults will be.

When planning a long trip with a friend, it is this sort of wisdom I bring to the table. My travel companion always wishes I had, instead, read the guidebook before the trip, instead of after, which is, I admit, a character flaw I have. But you'll never have to worry about bed-bugs if you stick with me.